WONDERS OF THE WORLD

Sunken Treasure

Debbie Levy

KIDHAVEN PRESS
An imprint of Thomson Gale, a part of The Thomson Corporation

THOMSON
GALE

Detroit • New York • San Francisco • San Diego • New Haven, Conn. • Waterville, Maine • London • Munich

© 2005 Thomson Gale, a part of The Thomson Corporation.

Thomson and Star Logo are trademarks and Gale and KidHaven Press are registered trademarks used herein under license.

For more information, contact
KidHaven Press
27500 Drake Rd.
Farmington Hills, MI 48331-3535
Or you can visit our Internet site at http://www.gale.com

ALL RIGHTS RESERVED.
No part of this work covered by the copyright hereon may be reproduced or used in any form or by any means—graphic, electronic, or mechanical, including photocopying, recording, taping, Web distribution or information storage retrieval systems—without the written permission of the publisher.

LIBRARY OF CONGRESS CATALOGING-IN-PUBLICATION DATA

Levy, Debbie.
  Sunken treasure / by Debbie Levy.
    p. cm. -- (Wonders of the world)
Contents: Sea full of treasure—The Spanish treasure fleet—Gold rush ship—Sunken city.
  Includes bibliographical references and index.
  ISBN 0-7377-2646-6 (alk. paper)
  I. Title. II. Wonders of the world

Printed in the United States of America

CONTENTS

4	CHAPTER ONE Sea Full of Treasure
13	CHAPTER TWO The Spanish Treasure Fleet
22	CHAPTER THREE Gold Rush Ship
30	CHAPTER FOUR Sunken City
38	Notes
39	Glossary
41	For Further Exploration
44	Index
47	Picture Credits
48	About the Author

CHAPTER ONE

Sea Full of Treasure

Before there is treasure, there is tragedy.

A ship leaves port at the beginning of a voyage. Its sails billow in the wind—or, at a later time in history, its engines churn noisily. **Cargo** is packed tightly in the hold. Sometimes a ship holds silver or gold coins or bars. Jewels such as emeralds and rubies may also be stashed on board.

Most ships reach their destinations safely, but others meet terrible dangers. Storms can whip the ocean into mountains of water. Even a large ship can be swamped when a watery peak comes crashing down on it or when its engines fail to drive it out of a deep valley of water. Storms are not the only danger. In some regions, icebergs loom unseen below the water's surface. In thick fog, the

CHAPTER ONE • **SEA FULL OF TREASURE**

captain and crew cannot see other ships or dangers, which can result in collisions.

Wrecks and Wealth

The loss of human life brought about by shipwrecks is tragic. The victims of a ship caught in a hurricane—passengers, captain, and crew—suffer horrible deaths. Their bodies are often never recovered.

Along with the suffering, however, comes opportunity. Lost cargoes can be found. Out of the tragedy of a shipwreck, treasure is born.

Ever since ships took to the seas, treasure hunters have found the lure of sunken cargo impossible to resist. Historians and **archaeologists** are also drawn to the watery

A human skull rests on a shipwreck in the Pacific Ocean. Shipwrecks can cause entire crews to lose their lives.

graves of ships to learn more about how people used to live and travel. One international organization estimates that 3 million shipwrecks are scattered across the globe.

All those shipwrecks could hold fortunes in gold, silver, jewels, and historical **artifacts**. In the 1500s, 1600s, and early 1700s, Spanish ships carried tons of gold and silver from the New World back to Spain. Large amounts of that precious cargo were lost at sea.

The age of treasure ships was not limited to the olden days of the Spanish American Empire. During World War I (1914–1918) and World War II (1939–1945), for example, governments in Europe shipped trillions of dollars in gold, silver, and other valuables to North America to escape the destruction of battles on their home soil. Some of these treasure ships ended up on the ocean floor.

From Disaster to Discovery

With the oceans full of treasure, one might expect that explorers are plucking gold off the seafloor every day. But the oceans do not give up their wealth so easily.

Most ships are wrecked in shallow water, less than several hundred feet down. Yet even these shipwrecks can remain hidden for years. After all, the oceans are vast. They take up 70 percent of the earth's surface. People have explored less than 1 percent of the bottom of this expanse. Shallow water is frequently found near coastlines, but this does not narrow the search much, as the earth's coastlines are 312,000 miles (504,000 kilometers) long—enough to go around the equator twelve times.

Of course, treasure hunters and archaeologists usually have an idea of where a ship went down. But ships

A scuba diver explores a shipwreck in the Florida Keys. Some shipwrecks hold fortunes in gold, silver, and jewels.

that sink in shallow water do not stay put. Storms, winds, and tides can carry pieces of a wreck miles from its first resting place.

Searching the Depths

In deep water, shipwrecks are more likely to remain in one place. But deep water hides its wrecks even better than the shallows, as the ocean's dark depths are difficult to explore.

To search out shipwrecks, scientists use **sonar**. A sonar machine on a ship sends out pulses of sound toward the ocean floor. The sound waves bounce off the floor and

WONDERS OF THE WORLD • **SUNKEN TREASURE**

travel back to the ship, creating a picture of the seabed. When the sound waves strike a formation such as an underwater mountain—or a shipwreck—the sonar map shows this as a "hit," or different pattern in the seabed.

Magnetometers are also used to discover sunken treasure. These are large magnets pulled through the water by a mother ship. The magnetometer creates an image that shows where metal—such as anchors, cannons, or the **hull** of a ship—rests on the seabed.

Using a handheld magnetometer, a scuba diver searches for buried treasure in the ocean floor.

CHAPTER ONE • SEA FULL OF TREASURE

Taking the Plunge

Sonar and magnetometers only show that a shipwreck might be lying on the ocean floor. To find out whether the sonar or magnetometer hit is really a shipwreck, people have to look at it.

Human beings were not designed to dive in thousands of feet of water. Sunlight does not penetrate deeper than 820 feet (250 meters). But darkness is the least of the challenges. The human body cannot withstand the tremendous weight of water that presses on a person when he or she dives deep underwater. Water is far heavier than air. At 3,300 feet (1,000 meters) underwater, pressure is one hundred times greater than it is on land. This is more than an unprotected human body can stand.

Despite the obstacles, people have plunged into the sea in search of treasure for thousands of years. Using no equipment, an experienced diver can hold his or her breath for several minutes and reach depths up to one hundred feet (thirty meters). But treasure recovery requires the ability to dive deeper and for longer periods of time.

In the 1800s, the first diving suits were developed to help divers explore the depths. The helmet was made of metal, and the body of canvas and rubber. A flexible tube ran from the helmet to an air supply on the deck of a ship.

Diving suits today are much lighter and more flexible. Also, divers now carry their air supply in tanks known as **scuba** gear on their backs. One new type of suit encases the diver in a lightweight hard shell filled

A diver trains for a deep-sea dive in a hard suit that can resist the great pressure of deep water.

with fluid to resist pressure. Wearing a hard suit, a diver can reach depths of 1,000 feet (305 meters) or more.

Submersibles and Robots

Even in a protective suit, a diver cannot safely dive deep enough to reach many of the wrecks at the bottom of the ocean. To reach greater depths, scientists have developed deep-diving vehicles called **submersibles**. Submersibles can withstand tremendous pressure. Their passengers travel deep below the surface wearing nothing more protective than ordinary clothes. Equipped with cameras and powerful lights, submersibles allow their

CHAPTER ONE • SEA FULL OF TREASURE

passengers to see and take pictures in the darkest depths. Submersibles also have mechanical arms and hooks to pick up items or moves things aside.

Yet even submersibles have limits. Although they can resist tremendous pressure, the pressure becomes overwhelming for passengers at depths beyond twenty thousand feet (six thousand meters). Also, as submersibles must be large enough to hold people, they cannot fit inside the small openings often found in shipwrecks.

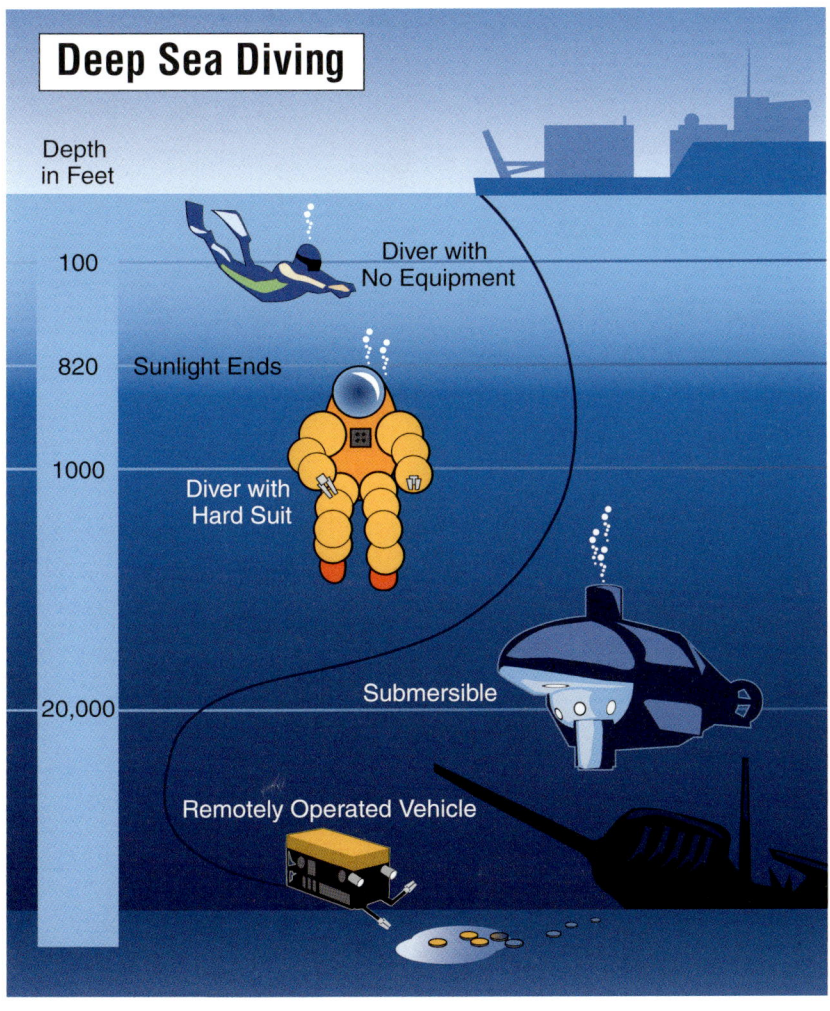

In response to these problems, scientists have developed deep-diving, unmanned robots called **remotely operated vehicles** (ROVs). Usually tied by a power cable to a mother ship, ROVs have mechanical arms, lights, and cameras. A person operates the robot using a controller similar to the joystick of a video game.

But exploring shipwrecks is not a game. Even with sonar, magnetometers, underwater cameras, scuba gear, submersibles, and robots, finding sunken treasure is hard work. The monetary rewards can be huge, but, as one expert wrote, "there are much more sensible routes to making quick money."[1] For many people, the challenge of the search and the chance to travel back in time through underwater exploration are the main attractions of treasure hunting—and they are as precious as gold.

The Spanish Treasure Fleet

Five hundred years ago, Spain was the most powerful country in Europe. Spanish settlers created colonies in North, Central, and South America. Before long, they found that the earth of this New World contained large amounts of gold, silver, and precious gemstones.

The king of Spain claimed much of the riches of the Americas. Private merchants also claimed a share. But getting the treasure back to Spain was difficult. Ships carrying such rich cargoes were at risk of attack by pirates.

To help reduce these risks, the Spanish government organized a special fleet of ships to carry treasure back to Spain. Large warships, called **galleons**, protected the smaller merchant ships in the treasure

WONDERS OF THE WORLD • SUNKEN TREASURE

Large warships called galleons, pictured in this sixteenth-century drawing, transported gold and silver across the Atlantic Ocean.

fleet. Galleons carried most of the fleet's gold and silver, while smaller vessels held farm products such as tobacco and indigo (a type of blue dye).

The 1622 Fleet

With twenty-eight ships, the 1622 fleet was not as large as some others, but its treasure was substantial. Its ships

CHAPTER TWO • THE SPANISH TREASURE FLEET

carried gold, silver, emeralds, and pearls. The fleet gathered in Havana, Cuba, and set sail for Spain on September 4, 1622. One galleon had the job of protecting the slow-sailing merchant ships in the rear. That ship was the *Nuestra Señora de Atocha*.

The *Atocha* was 112 feet (34 meters) long. It carried twenty bronze cannons and much more. According to the official papers drawn up before the fleet set sail, the *Atocha*'s cargo included 125 bars of gold, more than 1,000 **ingots** (blocks) of silver, 180,000 silver coins, 582 copper ingots, and 1,200 pounds (544 kilograms) of silverware.

A day after the fleet left Havana, a powerful hurricane struck. Unable to control their direction, the ships scattered across the water. Winds pushed the ships north toward the rocky reefs of Florida. Twenty of them were lucky enough to drift northwest. Most sailed out the storm in the Gulf of Mexico.

The *Atocha* was not among the lucky ships. Winds and waves pushed it closer and closer to the Florida reefs. On the morning of September 6, a huge wave dashed the *Atocha* onto the reef's jagged teeth. The angry seas tossed the ship about for a while longer, until it finally sank to the bottom. Out of 265 people on board, only 5 survived.

After the hurricane ended, the remaining ships of the treasure fleet returned to the scene of the storm to rescue survivors. All together, 550 people died in the lost ships.

Dreams of Treasure

For hundreds of years, stories of the lost ships of the Spanish treasure fleet sparked the imaginations of many people. One of these was Mel Fisher. Fisher grew up in Indiana, far

from any ocean, but he read about sunken treasure from the time he was a boy. Even while working on his family's chicken ranch as a young man, Fisher could not shake his dream of finding sunken treasure. In the 1960s, he and his wife and children moved to Florida so he could devote all his time to the search for Spanish treasure ships.

Fisher formed a treasure-hunting business. He raised money to pay for equipment, divers, and other crew members. People who gave money to his treasure business, called **investors**, were promised a share of his findings.

CHAPTER TWO • THE SPANISH TREASURE FLEET

After reading as much as possible about the fate of the 1622 treasure fleet, Fisher had good ideas about where the *Atocha* had sunk. He hired a historian to go to Spain to page through old papers that recorded the travels and cargoes of the treasure fleets. Such documents provided clues about what to look for in the search for the *Atocha*.

Another Tragedy

Fisher's search boats used sonar and magnetometers to detect structures on the ocean bottom. Scuba divers investigated areas where the sonar and magnetometers showed something promising. For a long time, Fisher and his crew did not find anything that was clearly from the *Atocha*. Months and years went by without success. Every day Fisher said to his crew, "Today's the day!"[2]

In 1975 Fisher's son Dirk recovered the *Atocha*'s cannons. That was an exciting moment. The old galleon seemed so near, and yet it remained hidden.

Then tragedy struck. Days after Dirk found the cannons, the search ship rolled over. Dirk Fisher, his wife, and a diver died in the accident. Three hundred fifty-three years after it went down, the *Atocha* claimed three more victims.

Atocha, at Last

The search continued, but the trail of the *Atocha* seemed to have gone cold. Then, in July 1985, Dirk's brother, Kane Fisher, was on a search boat 9 miles (14.5 kilometers) southeast of where the cannons had been found. Two divers swam down to investigate a hit on the magnetometer.

Soon, the divers surfaced excitedly. Fifty-five feet (16.7 meters) below the surface, they saw a reef made of countless silver coins, hundreds of silver bars, and hundreds of emeralds. "Put away the charts," Kane called back to his father, who was on land, "we've found the main pile!"[3]

Divers retrieved some silver bars to compare their markings to the records of the *Atocha*'s cargo. The markings matched. The *Atocha* had been found, thirty-five miles off the southwest tip of Florida.

Handle with Care

The *Atocha* team included a marine archaeologist who told the divers how to handle the shipwreck. First, divers laid a grid of pipes over the wreck. The grid's squares were numbered. This allowed everyone to identify exactly where items were found. Then divers made drawings and took photographs of each square in the grid.

Once divers had created detailed records of the site, they started to remove treasure. Divers filled baskets with artifacts, jewelry, coins, and other treasure, and people back on the boat pulled the baskets up.

The objects were fragile after lying in saltwater for more than 350 years. Experts had to use special methods, mostly chemical baths, to preserve the treasure from ruin. For example, silver coins and bars from the *Atocha* shipwreck had turned black from the minerals in seawater. Workers in laboratories on land placed them

In 1975 Dirk Fisher and his team raise one of the ten cannons from the wreck of the *Atocha*.

CHAPTER TWO • **THE SPANISH TREASURE FLEET**

in tanks of chemicals that softened the dark gunk on their surfaces. Later, workers scrubbed the silver clean and polished it to a beautiful gloss.

Another Treasure?

As divers removed one layer of artifacts and valuables, they discovered more underneath. They recovered thousands of emeralds that had not been listed in the ship's cargo records. The value of the *Atocha*'s treasure has been estimated at $400 million.

Mel Fisher and his wife, Dolores, display some of the gold objects recovered from the *Atocha* in 1985.

CHAPTER TWO • THE SPANISH TREASURE FLEET

Besides the treasure, divers recovered many items of historical interest. They found weapons, tools, dishes, seeds, and even insects. These items have helped historians and archaeologists understand more about how people lived in the early 1600s.

Fantastic as Mel Fisher's discovery was, it may be only part of the treasure the *Atocha* has to offer. Fisher's find included the hull, or bottom, of the galleon—but no evidence of the ship's upper deck, which probably washed away. Many believe the upper deck held its own treasure, perhaps as valuable as the treasure that has already been recovered. That treasure still awaits discovery.

CHAPTER
THREE

Gold Rush Ship

Just as the New World was like a vast treasure chest for Spain in the 1600s, California was a magnet for American treasure seekers after gold was discovered there in 1848. And just as the Spanish king brought his treasures home by ship, so did American gold miners, merchants, and bankers.

One ship, the U.S. mail steamship *Central America*, carried one-third of all the gold shipped east from California from 1852 to 1857. The *Central America* was 278 feet (85 meters) long, with steam engines powered by two large coal-burning furnaces. The engines drove paddle wheels that propelled the ship forward. The wooden ship sailed from Panama to New York once a month, often carrying passengers and cargo from California's gold rush country.

CHAPTER THREE • **GOLD RUSH SHIP**

Tons of Gold

In early September 1857 the *Central America* left Panama for its voyage to New York. It carried 475 passengers and 102 crew members under the command of Captain William Lewis Herndon. Many passengers carried gold coins, bars, nuggets, and dust, packed in baggage or tucked into treasure belts. Besides all this, the ship held mail and a cargo of more than three tons (three thousand kilograms) of gold bars and coins.

From Bad to Worse

The weather was hot and sunny as the *Central America* steamed toward Florida. At dinner one night, passengers at the captain's table talked about shipwrecks. Herndon said, "Well, I'll never survive my ship. If she goes down, I go under her **keel** [bottom]. But let us talk of something more cheerful."[4]

The next morning, Wednesday, September 9, the weather turned. By evening, a hurricane was brewing. The ship fought its way through mountains and valleys of water.

The fight became far more challenging on Friday, September 11. The engines were losing power. As a result, the ship's paddle wheels could not propel the ship through the churning seas. Also, the ship's **engineer** found a leak in the hull. The *Central America* was in great peril.

National Disaster

On Saturday, as the storm continued to pound, another ship came into view, the *Marine*. Herndon decided to

Many gold miners sailed home from California with their fortunes on mail ships like this one.

transfer as many passengers as possible to the much smaller *Marine*, women and children first. All afternoon, oarsmen rowed lifeboats through the waves to the *Marine*. By evening, all the women and children, and a few men, had been rowed to safety. But wind had separated the two ships by five miles (8.05 kilometers)—too far for the oarsmen to row anymore.

Back on the *Central America*, Herndon prepared for the worst. He told the crew to rip apart the upper deck so its pieces would serve as rafts for survivors. The passengers also prepared for the worst. They had to decide what to do with their gold. If they stuffed it into pockets, their treasure could become deadly. Gold is very heavy. A single gold brick could weigh down a strong swimmer. Knowing this, many threw their gold away.

CHAPTER THREE • **GOLD RUSH SHIP**

Sometime after 8:00 P.M. on Saturday, September 12, the *Central America* finally sank. Most of the men on board drowned. The following morning, a small boat, the *Ellen*, came upon survivors clutching their makeshift rafts. The *Ellen*'s crew pulled forty-nine men out of the sea alive. Herndon was not among the survivors.

News of the disaster spread throughout the country. The loss was one of the worst shipping disasters the nation had ever known, with 425 dead. Efforts to find the ship and its treasure failed.

All of the women and children aboard *Central America* were rowed to the safety of a nearby ship.

Into the Deep

More than one hundred years later, Thomas Thompson, an engineer from Columbus, Ohio, became interested in the *Central America*. He believed the ship had gone down in very deep water and that divers had been looking in the wrong places for years. Always interested in challenges, Thompson made deepwater work his mission and the *Central America* his goal.

Thompson assembled a team of ocean scientists and other experts. They raised money from investors to pay for equipment and crew. After reading everything they could about the shipwreck, Thompson and his team decided to search 1,400 square miles (2,253 square kilometers) of ocean—an area larger than Rhode Island. The water was too deep for divers and even too deep for people to explore comfortably in a submersible. Finding the *Central America* would be a job for a robot.

Nemo's Findings

For two summers starting in 1986, Thompson's group searched, using sonar, magnetometers, cameras, and an ROV lowered into the sea from a search boat. They found sites that looked like shipwrecks, but none included a paddle wheel. Toward the end of the third summer, the team headed to a new site they identified on their sonar maps. Thompson and the others were eager to try out their new underwater robot, Nemo. Thompson had built the robot specifically for recovering sunken treasure, with an "arm" that could bend and reach in all different directions.

The crew launched Nemo, attached to a very long cable, and waited while it approached the ocean bottom.

A crab scurries away from an ROV. Thomas Thompson used a similar ROV to locate the *Central America*.

Then the search began, using sonar and Nemo's video camera. Soon the sonar registered a hit, and another, and another. Then, "Whoa!" said the team's photographer, who was watching a video monitor. "We've got a biggie here!"[5]

Exactly 131 years earlier, on September 11, 1857, the *Central America* had begun taking on water, which eventually made its big paddle wheels grind to a halt. And now, the video showed a rusting paddle wheel lying flat, 8,000 feet (2,438 meters) underwater.

Garden of Gold

Nemo's video pictures showed the ocean floor littered with dishes and bottles. A ship's bell sat in the muck. The ROV brought the solid bronze bell to the surface. The bell's markings showed it was from the *Central America*.

WONDERS OF THE WORLD • **SUNKEN TREASURE**

But a bell of bronze was not a cargo of gold. Days and weeks passed, with technicians hoping to see gold on their video monitors. Then, one day, Nemo's operator sent a stream of water toward the ocean bottom to blow away mud. The photographer adjusted Nemo's lights. "Suddenly," Thompson later wrote, "the same monitors that had revealed nothing but colorless ocean terrain for weeks now appeared to be painted brilliant gold."[6]

Gold bars were stacked neatly as if on store shelves. Others were spread across the ocean floor. Gold coins rose from the floor in towers. The team called the area the "Garden of Gold."

Items recovered from the *Central America* include bars, bricks, and coins of gold.

CHAPTER THREE • GOLD RUSH SHIP

For weeks, Nemo flew all around the shipwreck, taking video and still pictures. When winter weather rolled in, the expedition came to a halt for the season. Recovering the treasure would have to wait.

The next summer, Thompson and his team returned to the site to retrieve treasure. Nemo picked up large gold bars with its padded "fingers." It retrieved individual coins with a suction picker—basically, a rubber cup at the end of Nemo's arm. The robot put these items in its storage drawers. To recover clumps of coins without scratching them, technicians used a machine that encased each clump in a rubbery substance called silicone. A member of the team invented this machine just for the purpose of picking up the *Central America*'s coins.

Finding History

Up to now, Thompson had kept the find a secret. At the end of the summer exploration season in 1989, he announced the discovery publicly. Among the people gathered to hear the announcement were twenty-nine people related to passengers of the *Central America*.

The treasure recovered from the wreck of the *Central America* was worth more than $100 million. Those involved in the search for the old steamer were thrilled about the riches, but their deepest thrill was not about money and wealth. As Thompson wrote: "This was the very gold that drew people to California and fueled the nation's economy in the mid-19th century. . . . Part of our American heritage, this was history in the form of a national treasure. And we had found it."[7]

CHAPTER
FOUR

Sunken City

Shipwrecks account for most of the world's sunken treasures. But there is another source of treasure lost to the ocean. Towns and cities across the globe have been swallowed up by the sea in floods and earthquakes or gradually drowned by rises in ocean levels. One such sunken city is Port Royal, Jamaica.

Wickedest City

The island of Jamaica became a colony of Great Britain in 1655. Its largest town, Port Royal, was built around a harbor on the island's southeast coast. By the late 1600s, Port Royal was the biggest and busiest British port in the New World, with Boston, Massachusetts, a close second.

Much of the business activity in Port Royal concerned trade in sugar and other products of the Caribbean Sea

CHAPTER FOUR • SUNKEN CITY

region. Slave traders also worked in Port Royal, selling and buying enslaved people who had been transported from Africa. In addition, many pirates used Port Royal as a base from which they launched attacks on ships in the Caribbean. They came to the town to relax, eat, drink, gamble, and make merry. Because of this, Port Royal's nickname was the "wickedest city in the world."

Disaster Strikes

Tuesday, June 7, 1692, the weather in Port Royal was mild. People went about their normal business. Late in the morning, before noon, some stopped at a tavern for the midday meal. They were not to enjoy it.

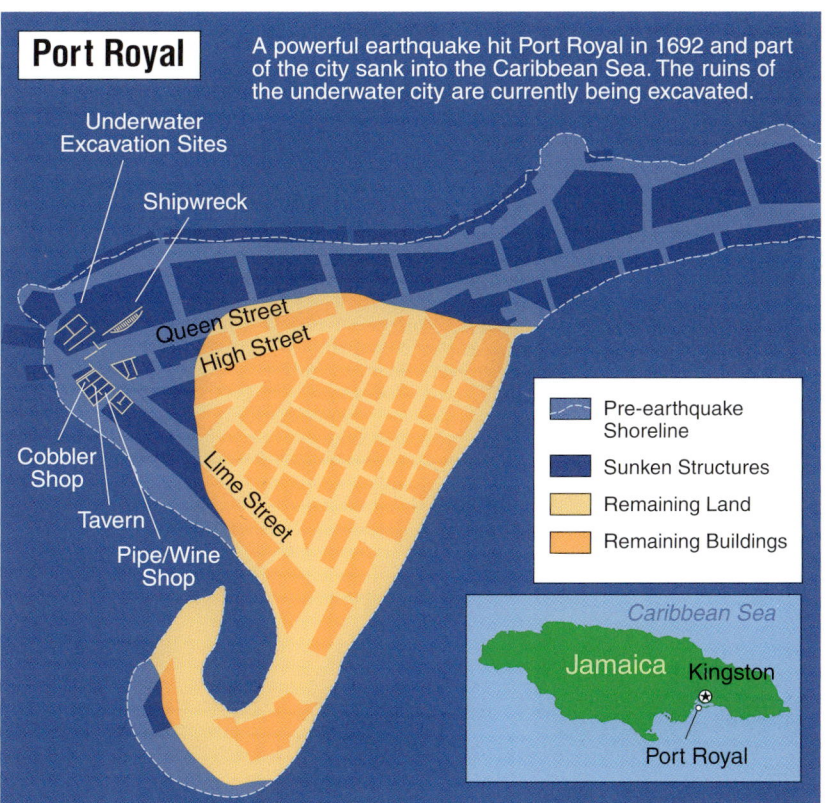

A powerful earthquake hit Port Royal in 1692 and part of the city sank into the Caribbean Sea. The ruins of the underwater city are currently being excavated.

WONDERS OF THE WORLD • SUNKEN TREASURE

Many pirates like these and their treasures were lost when the coastal city of Port Royal sank in 1692.

The Reverend Emmanuel Heath, leader of the Church of England in Port Royal, was one of the townspeople who had stopped at a tavern. As he sat at a table, he felt the floor shaking beneath his feet. A powerful earthquake had struck Port Royal.

CHAPTER FOUR • SUNKEN CITY

Heath ran from the tavern and headed away from the town's center. He ran far enough away to survive, but he saw what happened to those who were not as lucky: "Some were swallowed up to the Neck, and then the Earth shut upon them; and squeezed them to death; and in that manner several are left buried with their Heads above ground."[8] Approximately two thousand people were killed immediately, out of a total population of sixty-five hundred to eight thousand. Several thousand more died over the following days. Much of the town was now at the bottom of the sea. The entire tragedy took only a few minutes.

Buried in Mud

In the years that followed the destruction of Port Royal, stories were told of the city of gold at the bottom of the sea, a city filled with chests of pirate treasure. Treasure hunters started searching for this fantastic wealth almost immediately after the earthquake, but they did not find it.

The first organized scientific expedition to uncover Port Royal had its beginnings in 1956, 264 years after the earthquake. That year, archaeologist Edwin A. Link visited the site with his wife, Marion Clayton Link. Diving down to the site of the underwater city was not difficult, as the ocean was only 20 to 40 feet (7 to 12 meters) deep. But the Links found that the city was covered in 4 to 6 feet (1.2 to 1.8 meters) of mud. Special tools would be required to dig out enough mud to unearth even small parts of the city.

Link was not discouraged. During the next two years, he designed and built a special ship, the *Sea Diver*, to explore the sunken city. The ship included an electrical system powerful enough to operate a large airlift, or dredge. The airlift was like a giant vacuum cleaner to suck up mud and gravel from the ocean floor. Link also included a powerful jetting hose to shoot clear water at portions of the sunken city and help divers examine what lay before them.

Leftover Stew

In the spring of 1959, the expedition was ready. Divers joined the Links on the *Sea Diver*, which motored to the site of the underwater city. The airlift sat on its own barge, tied alongside the main ship. The giant vacuum noisily started sucking up mud and gravel from the ocean bottom. The crew aimed the airlift's end toward the barge deck so material brought up from the bottom would fall there, where members of the expedition could examine it.

Before long, the remains of the drowned city began spewing in the air. The airlift spit up bricks, broken bottles, dishes, coal, and roof tiles. Divers descended into the water to work near the mouth of the airlift hose. As the vacuum sucked away silt, they retrieved artifacts too delicate to be suctioned up in the hose, such as pewter spoons, a brass ladle, and old rum bottles.

Divers also used a metal detector to guide them toward areas where the airlift would be most likely to uncover artifacts. With the help of the metal detectors, divers uncovered a copper cooking pot, filled with mud. The pot also held a surprise—animal bones. "Why, a stew must have been cooking for dinner when the earth-

CHAPTER FOUR • **SUNKEN CITY**

quake struck,"⁹ said Link to his fellow explorers. As they brought up more plates, spoons, candlesticks, bottles, and a fireplace grill, they realized that they had been excavating a tavern kitchen.

Edwin A. Link and his team used a powerful jetting hose like this one to remove sand from the sunken city.

Time for Tragedy

For ten weeks, the *Sea Diver* expedition explored Port Royal. Divers retrieved hundreds more items. The most interesting artifact was a pocket watch, spewed up by the airlift. The watch's hands were missing, but they had left an imprint, detectable by X-ray photography, on a piece of coral that had formed over the face of the clock. The hands showed the time to be 11:43—seventeen minutes before 12:00 noon. The watch had stopped at the moment of the earthquake, either broken by the force of the quake or drowned by the ocean. It was a silent reminder of the tragedy that occurred there on June 7, 1692.

Following the Link expedition, other divers and archaeologists continued to unearth large parts of Port Royal. Divers have recovered tens of thousands of artifacts. Homes, businesses, and ships wrecked in the harbor at the time of the earthquake have all been identified in the murky water of the drowned city. Thanks to all these findings, Jamaican archaeologists and historians are able to understand more about their country's early days.

And although divers did discover silver coins in the underwater city, they have not found the fabled pirates' treasure chests of gold—at least, not yet.

Tomorrow's Treasures

One day in the future, other coastal cities may suffer the same fate as Port Royal. And although ships today are safer than vessels of the past, storms continue to swallow them up and drag them to the bottom of the sea.

Hoping to find sunken treasure, explorers will continue to search for shipwrecks across the globe.

Today, however, few ships carry treasure in the form of gold, silver, or jewels. These valuables are more likely to be transported by airplane. Also, gold and silver are no longer as important to trade as they were in the past. Once these metals were the foundation of the world's money supply, but modern nations no longer base their money on gold or silver.

In some ways, then, the era of sunken treasure is over. But there is enough treasure still hidden in the ocean to keep treasure hunters busy for many, many years.

Notes

Chapter One: Sea Full of Treasure
1. Nigel Pickford, *The Atlas of Ship Wrecks and Treasure.* New York: Dorling Kindersley, 1994, p. 9.

Chapter Two: The Spanish Treasure Fleet
2. Quoted in Mel Fisher, Maritime Heritage Society and Museum, "Mel's Story," www.melfisher.org/melstory.htm.
3. Quoted in Mel Fisher, Maritime Heritage Society and Museum, "Mel's Story."

Chapter Three: Gold Rush Ship
4. Quoted in Gary Kinder, *Ship of Gold in the Deep Blue Sea.* New York: Atlantic Monthly Press, 1998, p. 24.
5. Quoted in Kinder, *Ship of Gold in the Deep Blue Sea*, p. 425.
6. Thomas G. Thompson, "America's Lost Treasure," www.sscentralamerica.com.
7. Thompson, "America's Lost Treasure."

Chapter Four: Sunken City
8. Quoted in Larry Gragg, "The Port Royal Earthquake," *History Today*, September 2000, p. 28.
9. Quoted in Marion Clayton Link, "Exploring the Drowned City of Port Royal," *National Geographic*, February 1960, pp. 151, 172.

Glossary

archaeologist: A person who is trained in archaeology, or the investigation of history by recovering and examining artifacts and other items left by people and cultures of the past.

artifact: An object of historical interest.

cargo: Goods carried by a ship.

engineer: A person who is trained in engineering, or the use of science and math to create or improve projects and inventions, such as building structures or machines.

galleon: A large Spanish warship, used from the 1400s to the 1700s.

hull: The main structure of a ship.

ingot: A bar or block of metal.

investor: A person who provides money to a project or business with the expectation of receiving a greater amount of money in return as a result of the success of the project or business.

keel: The bottom of a ship.

magnetometer: A device that finds metal by detecting magnetic fields.

remotely operated vehicle: An unmanned robot, also called an ROV, used to explore the deep ocean.

scuba: A portable breathing device used by divers for breathing underwater; from the words *s*elf-*c*ontained *u*n-derwater *b*reathing *a*pparatus.

sonar: A device that uses sound waves to create a map of the floor of a body of water and to find objects underwater.

submersible: A ship that operates underwater.

For Further Exploration

Books

Robert D. Ballard, *Exploring the Titanic*. New York: Scholastic, 1988. The scientist who found the famous passenger ship RMS *Titanic*, which sunk on April 14, 1912, tells the story of the sinking and his discovery. Photographs, pictures, and diagrams illustrate the story.

Robert D. Ballard and Rick Archbold, *Ghost Liners*. New York: Little, Brown, 1998. In words, photographs, and paintings, the famous oceanographer Robert D. Ballard takes the reader on a tour of famous ships that have been lost at sea. The ships are not treasure ships but ocean liners that carried passengers.

Frances Dipper, *The New Book of Treasures Under the Ocean*. Brookfield, CT: Copper Beech, 1997. Filled with large pictures, this book looks at the technology of underwater exploration, shipwrecks, treasure hunts, and more.

Anita Ganeri, *The Oceans Atlas*. New York: Dorling Kindersley, 1994. In colorful detail, this atlas explores the world's oceans. Subjects include the terrain of the ocean, ocean exploration, undersea life, and ocean archaeology.

Gail Gibbons, *Exploring the Deep, Dark Sea*. New York: Little, Brown, 1999. The reader is taken on a voyage deep underwater in a submersible. How the submersible operates, and the type of work it accomplishes underwater are explored.

———, *Sunken Treasure*. New York: Thomas Y. Crowell, 1988. This book is mainly about the search for the treasure ship *Nuestra Señora de Atocha*, with brief discussions of four other treasure ships.

Sandra Markle, *Pioneering Ocean Depths*. New York: Atheneum Books for Young Readers, 1995. This book explains how scientists explore the ocean and some of the discoveries they have made from their explorations.

Nigel Pickford, *The Atlas of Ship Wrecks and Treasure*. New York: Dorling Kindersley, 1994. This is a book and atlas in one, with illustrated stories of some of the world's most interesting shipwrecks plus a section with maps that show the location of more than fourteen hundred shipwrecks.

Web sites

Ocean Explorer (http://oceanexplorer.noaa.gov). This site is sponsored by the U.S. National Oceanic and Atmospheric Administration. It describes current and recent NOAA ocean explorations involving shipwrecks, geology, and underwater life. Includes detailed information and pictures of ships, submersibles, diving equipment, sonar, and other tools used in underseas expeditions.

The Port Royal Project (http://nautarch.tamu.edu/portroyal/index.htm). The Nautical Archaeology Program of Texas A&M University created this Web site to present information about its work uncovering the sunken city of Port Royal, Jamaica. Underwater photographs and detailed diagrams show what excavating an underwater city is really like.

Woods Hole Oceanographic Institution (www.whoi.edu). Woods Hole is a research and education center for ocean science. Its Web site includes interactive tours of an ocean research ship, the *Atlantis*, and of a submersible, the *Alvin*.

Index

airlifts, 33–34
archaeologists, 5–6, 18
Atocha (ship), 15, 17–18, 20–21

California, 22
cargo, 4
Central America (steamship), 22
  found, 26–27
  sunk, 23–25
  treasure of, 28–29

deaths
  of divers, 17
  in Port Royal, 33
  in shipwrecks, 5, 15, 25
deep water, 7
divers
  deaths of, 17
  water pressure and, 9, 11
  see also deaths; individual divers

diving gear, 9–10

earthquakes, 32–33
Ellen (boat), 25
equipment
  airlifts, 33–34
  diving gear, 9–10
  magnetometers, 8, 17
  metal detectors, 34
  remotely operated vehicles (ROVs), 12, 26–29
  sonar, 7–8, 17, 27
  submersibles, 10–11

Fisher, Dirk, 17
Fisher, Kane, 17–18
Fisher, Mel, 15–18, 20–21
fog, 4

galleons, 13–14, 15
"Garden of Gold," 28
gold rush, 22

Heath, Emmanuel, 32–33
Herndon, William Lewis, 23–25
historians, 5–6, 17
hurricanes, 5, 15, 23

icebergs, 4

Link, Edwin A., 33–36
Link, Mary Clayton, 33–36

magnetometers, 8, 17
mail steamships, 22
Marine (ship), 23–24
metal detectors, 34

Nemo, 26–29
Nuestra Señora de Atocha (ship), 15, 17–18, 20–21

oceans, 7

Port Royal (Jamaica), 30–31
  deaths in, 33
  destroyed, 31–33
  treasures, 34–36
  uncovered, 33–34

remotely operated vehicles (ROVs), 12, 26–29
robots. *See* Nemo; remotely operated vehicles (ROVs)

scuba gear, 9
Sea Diver (ship), 33–34
shallow water, 6–7
shipwrecks
  causes of, 4–5, 15, 23
  deaths in, 5, 25
  number of, 6
1622 Spanish fleet, 14
sonar, 7–8, 17, 27
Spanish American empire, 6, 13–15
storms, 4
  see also hurricanes
submersibles, 10–11

Thompson, Thomas, 26–29
treasure
  of *Atocha*, 18, 20–21

of *Central America*,
  28–29
of Port Royal, 34–36
treasure-hunting
  business, 16, 26

water pressure, 9, 11
"wickedest city in the
  world," 31
World War I, 6
World War II, 6

Picture Credits

Cover Image: © Jonathan Blair/CORBIS
© Art Today, Inc., 7, 14, 37
© Hal Beral/CORBIS, 5
© Bettmann/CORBIS, 19
© Jonathan Blair/CORBIS, 20
Chris Jouan, 11, 16, 31
© Amos Nachoum/CORBIS, 8, 10
North Wind Picture Archives, 24, 25, 12
© Jeffrey L. Rotman/CORBIS, 35
Time Life Pictures/Getty Images, 28
© Ralph White/CORBIS, 27

About the Author

Before she started writing books for children, Debbie Levy practiced law with a large Washington, D.C., law firm and worked as a newspaper editor. She has a bachelor's degree in government and foreign affairs from the University of Virginia and a law degree and master's degree in world politics from the University of Michigan. Her most recent books for KidHaven Press and its sister press, Blackbirch Press, are about slave life, Maryland, and the Berlin Wall. She has also published books for young people on topics ranging from bigotry to medical ethics to the Vietnam War. Debbie enjoys paddling around in kayaks and canoes and fishing in the Chesapeake Bay region. She lives with her husband, two sons, dog, and cat in Maryland.